INVESTIGATE EARTH SCIENCE

Kathy Furgang

CANYONS

E | **Enslow Publishing**
101 W. 23rd Street
Suite 240
New York, NY 10011
USA
enslow.com

Words to Know

crust The earth's outer layer.

earthquake A sudden shaking of the earth's crust.

erosion The movement of rocks and other materials in the earth.

plate A section of the earth's crust, or outer layer.

sediment Material such as rocks, dirt, and sand that is left behind by water or wind.

species A group of similar living things that share certain traits.

submersible A boat that is used for exploring underwater areas.

weathering The breakdown of rocks and other materials in the earth.

Contents

Canyons Tell a Story

A canyon is much more than a big hole in the ground. Every canyon on the planet tells its own rocky story about the earth's history. Many canyons take millions of years to form. And no canyon is ever done forming. The earth continues to shape canyons. Canyons get deeper and wider over time.

What's in a Name?

Canyons are sometimes called ravines, gullies, or gorges.

Canyons represent millions of years of changes in the earth.

Creating a Canyon

How do canyons form? Water and wind play a big part in the story. **Weathering** is the breaking apart of rocks and other materials. Wind can weather rocks over time. Tiny pieces of rock break apart. They hit into other rocks. These rocks slowly break down.

Water can also cause weathering. Water gets into cracks in rocks. The water expands when it freezes. When this happens again and again, the rock breaks apart.

Wind and water slowly broke down the earth to create the Fish River Canyon.

Rivers run through many canyons, carving the rock out over time.

Getting Carried Away

Erosion is the next step of the process. Erosion is the movement of weathered material. Rain and wind carry away bits of weathered rock, dirt, sand, and soil. Rainwater carves a path of weathered rock. Erosion forms a river over time. The river gets wider and deeper. More rocks crumble, fall, and get carried away. Eventually, a canyon is formed.

Learning from the Layers

When you look into a canyon, you can learn more about the earth. The sides of canyon walls can show how **sediment**, or eroded material, settled and formed into layers of rock.

The earth's outer layer is called the **crust**. It is made of solid rock. But the crust is not one big piece that goes around the whole world. It is broken into sections called **plates**. These plates shift and move. The plates even collide, or hit into each other. When this happens, one plate might shift upward. The other plate gets pushed below. This type of movement can also form canyons.

A Grand View

One of the most famous canyons in the world is the Grand Canyon, in Arizona. To see this entire canyon in one day, you could hop into a helicopter. It is 277 miles (446 kilometers) long

The walls of Palo Duro Canyon in Texas show the layers of sediment that settled as the canyon formed.

and about 18 miles (29 km) wide. The Colorado River is at the bottom of the canyon. Watch your step if you decide to walk to the bottom. The canyon is 6,000 feet (1,800 meters) deep.

Slow and Steady

The Grand Canyon has been getting deeper each year by about the thickness of a sheet of paper. In one hundred years, that's about the thickness of a pack of notebook paper.

Canyon Life

Even though canyons are rocky areas, there is still plenty of life there. The Grand Canyon, for example, is home to 91 known **species** of mammals. These include coyotes, raccoons, and mountain lions. More

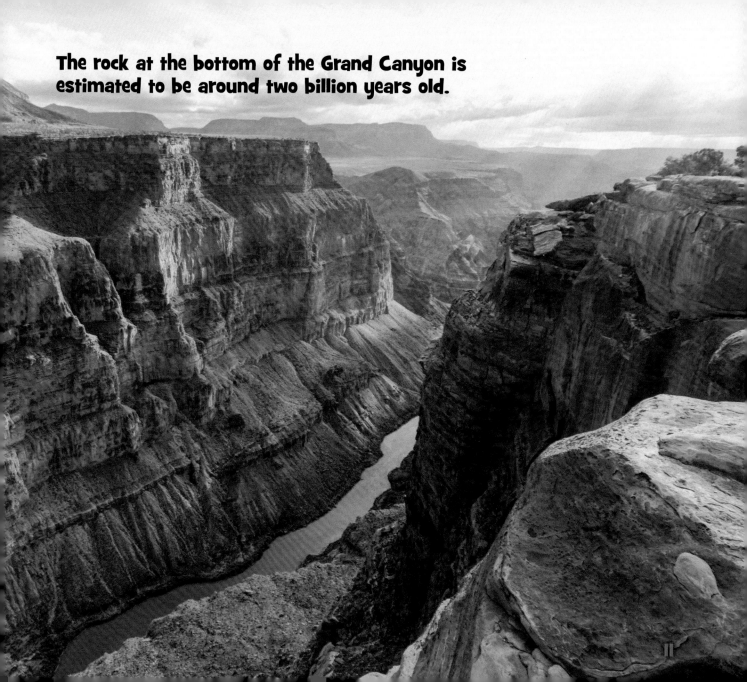

The rock at the bottom of the Grand Canyon is estimated to be around two billion years old.

11

The Native American group the Anasazi lived in these cliff dwellings. Today, the area is Canyon de Chelly National Monument in Arizona.

than 440 species of birds live there. And over 1,700 kinds of plants can be found in the canyon.

Even people make homes in canyons. More than a thousand years ago, one group of Native Americans built homes right into canyon walls. Today, that area in the American Southwest is still used by the Navajo Indians.

Submarine Canyons

Not all canyons are dry like a desert. Some are soaking wet! Submarine canyons are underwater valleys. They form at the edge of a high, rocky shoreline. Submarine canyons are often long and narrow. They curve and bend like a river.

Like most canyons, submarine canyons can form slowly over time. But many form quickly! An **earthquake** is a sudden movement

La Jolla submarine canyon is off the coast of La Jolla, California.

The map shows the underwater area where La Jolla Canyon is located.

of the earth's crust. An earthquake can cause a crack that can quickly form an underwater canyon. Huge storms with crashing waves can also break through the crust. Rushing water and sediment work quickly to cause erosion. Water fills the underground space. Eventually it becomes a home for marine life.

Diving Deep

Some submersibles explore the deep sea, where humans cannot go. The deepest part of the ocean is called the Challenger Deep. It is 36,070 feet (10,994 m) below the ocean surface.

Submersibles like this one bring back important information about underwater areas.

Canyon Exploration

Above ground, we can simply walk through a canyon to observe it. Submarine canyons are much different. They are much harder to get to. Divers can only explore small parts of these underground spaces. The areas get too dangerous for people to explore.

Underwater Discoveries

A submersible is a vehicle that can explore underwater areas. Some are like robots, controlled by humans above ground. The submersibles can take photos. They can measure the spaces they move through. They can even collect rock or other sediment. Scientists learn a lot about submarine canyons with the help of submersibles.

Record-Breaking Canyons

What's the deepest canyon in the world? What about the longest? Both of those records belong to the same canyon! The Yarlung Tsangpo Grand Canyon is in Tibet, China. It is 313 miles (504 km) long. The deepest part of the canyon is 19,714 feet (6,008 m) deep.

This huge canyon was formed when the earth's plates shifted. One plate moved up. This made a river's path steeper than before. More erosion occurred as a result. Over time, the river canyon became longer and deeper. It even bends around a mountain.

Tibet's Yarlung Tsangpo Grand Canyon is the deepest canyon in the world.

19

Going to Extremes

The Yarlung Tsangpo Grand Canyon is so long that it passes through different climate regions. The highest temperatures in the mountain areas barely get above freezing. In lower areas, temperatures can get above 100 degrees Fahrenheit (37 degrees Celsius).

Fastest-Forming Canyons

Which of the world's canyons has formed the fastest? It's not possible to know for sure. However, one canyon in Texas might win the prize. Lake Canyon Gorge formed in just three days! This very rare event happened in 2002. First, heavy rains caused a lake in the area to flood. The water spilled into a nearby river. The heavy flooding lasted for weeks. Debris

Lake Canyon Gorge is 23 feet (7 meters) deep.

and sediment blocked the river's path. With nowhere else to go, the heavy sediment carved out the gorge in just a few days.

This new gorge taught scientists a lot. They learned that other gorges may have formed this way. Instead of being a slow process, some gorges or canyons may have formed quickly.

This land feature, like many other canyons, also gives people a great place to visit nature.

Activity: Make a Canyon Model

●●● You can make your own model of a canyon!
You will need:

- aluminum cake pan
- plastic lid for a rectangular container
- stones or gravel, mixed with wet sand
- one cup measuring cup
- pitcher of water
- an adult

1. Work outside on the ground. Have an adult cut a one-inch hole in one of the short sides of the cake pan. Place one end of the lid on the pan's other short end to make a "hill" going into the pan.

2. Cover the bottom of the pan and hill with several inches of gravel and sand. Pat it down evenly.

3. Pour a cup of water very slowly from the top of the hill.

4. Predict how long it will take for the entire pitcher of water to carve a stream to the bottom of the pan. Try it.

5. How much wider will the stream get if you pour another pitcher of water? Try it.

6. Now try to make a deeper canyon. Start with twice as much gravel and sand.

●●● Learn More

Books

Chin, Jason. *Grand Canyon*. New York, NY: Roaring Brook Press, 2017.

Marsted, Melissa. *Buzzy and the Red Rock Canyons: Utah's National Parks*. Park City, UT: Lucky Penny, 2016.

Peter, Carsten. *Extreme Planet: Carsten Peter's Adventures in Volcanoes, Caves, Canyons, Deserts, and Beyond!* Washington, DC: National Geographic Children's Books, 2015.

Websites

Grand Canyon: National Parks Service
www.nps.gov/grca/learn/kidsyouth/fact-sheets.htm
Visit the Grand Canyon website of the National Parks Service.

Grand Canyon West
www.grandcanyonwest.com
Find out what you can do in the canyon, including visiting the Skywalk viewing platform, 4,000 feet above the canyon.

National Park Foundation
www.nationalparks.org/our-work/programs/npf-kids
Check out videos, activities, and maps to learn about the parks, including the canyons that are part of the national parks system.

●●● Index

Published in 2020 by Enslow Publishing, LLC.
101 W. 23rd Street, Suite 240, New York, NY 10011

Library of Congress Cataloging-in-Publication Data
Names: Furgang, Kathy, author.
Title: Canyons / Kathy Furgang. Description: New York : Enslow Publishing, 2020. | Series: Investigate earth science | Includes bibliographical references and index. | Audience: K to Grade 4.
Identifiers: LCCN 2018046196| ISBN 9781978507425 (library bound) | ISBN 9781978508590 (pbk.) | ISBN 9781978508606 (6 pack)
Subjects: LCSH: Canyons—Juvenile literature.
Classification: LCC GB562 .F87 2020 | DDC 551.44/2—dc23
LC record available at https://lccn.loc.gov/2018046196

Printed in the United States of America

To Our Readers: We have done our best to make sure all website addresses in this book were active and appropriate when we went to press. However, the author and the publisher have no control over and assume no liability for the material available on those websites or on any websites they may link to. Any comments or suggestions can be sent by e-mail to customerservice@enslow.com.